HOCKEY SUPERSTARS

CHAMPION NHL
Defensemen

BY

James Duplacey

A Beech Tree Paperback Book
NEW YORK

Text copyright © 1997 by NHL Enterprises, Inc.; and Dan Diamond and Associates, Inc.
First published in Canada by Kids Can Press,
29 Birch Avenue, Toronto, Ontario, Canada M4V 1E2

ISBN 0-688-15688-6
First Beech Tree Edition, 1997
10 9 8 7 6 5 4 3 2 1

Photo credits
All photos **Bruce Bennett Studios**, except: **Boston Public Library, Print Department**: 17 (left). **Frank Prazak Collection / Hockey Hall of Fame**: 10 (bottom), 16 (both), 21 (top and right), back cover (left). **Graphic Artists Collection / Hockey Hall of Fame**: cover (front left), 10 (top), 20, 21 (bottom left). **Imperial Oil Turofsky Collection / Hockey Hall of Fame**: 7 (both), 17 (right), 24 (left).

CONTENTS

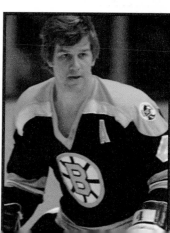

Swoooossh

Setting up behind his own net, the defenseman scans the ice surface stretching out in front of him. Out of the corner of his eye he spots an opposing forward streaking down the left side, so he swings sharply to the right and heads up ice. He moves the puck as if it's glued to his stick, gliding over the blue line searching for an open man. Spotting his center through a swirling maze of jerseys, he feathers a perfect cross-ice pass to him. It would be exciting to join in the rush, but for the good of the team he decides to reverse and drop back to protect his own zone. The entire play took less than ten seconds, and the defenseman will have to make similar decisions many times each game. Every choice holds its own dangers and rewards.

Defensemen are much more than strongmen who muscle players off the puck or hand out punishing bodychecks. They also bear the responsibility for the whole game on their broad shoulders. Often asked to play 30 minutes a game, a defenseman must constantly shift focus and adapt to the pace of the play. Since one wrong move can spell the difference between victory and defeat, it takes a special player to excel under such pressure. The defensemen honored here have shown they have the courage and skill to compete at the highest level. They are truly champion defensemen.

Viacheslav Fetisov (*top left*) was one of the first Russian players to join the NHL.

Ray Bourque (*top right*) has been the NHL's top defenseman since he entered the league. He was invited to play in his fifteenth All-Star Game in 1997.

Joe Watson (*far left*) was a regular on the Flyer blue line for 11 seasons.

Al MacInnis (*left*) was delighted in 1989 when he won the Conn Smythe Trophy as most valuable player in the playoffs.

Number 4, Bobby Orr (*right*) used his outstanding speed and stickhandling ability to change the way the position of defense is played.

POWER AND PRIDE

Ed Jovanovski

Florida

Even during his rookie season, Ed Jovanovski played with the poise of a veteran. This 6'2'' rearguard clears the puck quickly and confidently from his own zone, and is one of the best in the league at moving players from in front of his own net.

Jovanovski makes his biggest impact with his bodychecking. Because of his solid build and powerful legs, he can deliver bruising bodychecks and still keep his balance. That allows Jovanovski to pick up loose pucks and start offensive attacks. In his first NHL season, Jovanovski was named to the NHL All-Rookie Team and was a finalist for the rookie-of-the-year award.

"He could be the hardest-hitting defenseman in the NHL right now."
BOBBY CLARKE, 1996
Philadelphia Flyers general manager

During the 1995–96 playoffs, Jovanovski led all rookies in assists and shots on goal, and tied for most points by a rookie.

Doug Harvey

Montreal, NY Rangers, Detroit, St. Louis

The secret to Doug Harvey's success in the NHL was his ability to control the pace of the play. Playing defense allowed Harvey to be involved in all aspects of the game. He used his speed and pinpoint passing to lead offensive surges. And since Harvey was a powerful bodychecker and clever stickhandler, he could break up enemy attacks or clear the crease in his own zone.

Harvey played 22 seasons of pro hockey in three leagues. He won the Norris Trophy as the NHL's top rearguard 7 times and was named to 11 league All-Star teams. In 1992, Harvey was named to the NHL's 75th Anniversary All-Time All-Star Team.

"When you look back to the great Canadiens teams in the fifties, the dominant person on the ice was Doug Harvey. Doug was a true team man. He wasn't selfish at all."

TOM JOHNSON, 1992
Montreal Canadiens defenseman

Harvey was inducted into the Hockey Hall of Fame in 1973.

Brothers on the Blue Line

Derian Hatcher

Minnesota, Dallas

Kevin Hatcher

Washington, Dallas, Pittsburgh

When Derian and Kevin Hatcher played together for Dallas, they were known as the Twin Towers because of their size, strength, and stamina. Derian can block shots, cut off the passing lanes, or muscle a forward into the boards. Although he is best known for his defensive work, Derian scored a pair of key goals in Team USA's victory over Canada in the 1996 World Cup of Hockey.

Older brother Kevin is also known for his physical presence. His powerful skating allows him to break through the opposition and set up goals for his team. Thanks to his quick, accurate shot, Kevin is one of only seven defensemen in NHL history to score 30 goals in a season.

Derian (left) and Kevin (right) Hatcher

"They complement each other, they really do. I think you can see that out there— they seem to know where each other is."
CRAIG LUDWIG, 1995
Teammate

Jimmy Watson
Philadelphia

Joe Watson
Boston, Philadelphia, Colorado Rockies

In their six seasons together with the Philadelphia Flyers, Jimmy and Joe Watson helped the Flyers win a pair of Stanley Cup titles and finish in first place four times. While both men played a tough, physical game, they had different styles. Joe preferred to stay in his own end zone, preventing goals rather than trying to score them. He was also an outspoken leader with a powerful voice.

A gifted skater and playmaker, Jimmy played a more offensive style. Known as a "heads-up" player, he relied on his brain as much as his muscles. Jimmy's smart approach to the game helped him play with a confidence that earned him five trips to the NHL All-Star Game in his ten-year career.

Jimmy Watson, left, played his entire ten-year career with Philadelphia while brother Joe, above, played 11 of his 14 seasons with the Flyers.

"They intimidate the opposition, really throw them off their game. They just come to play every day. What more can you ask?"

PAT QUINN, 1978
Philadelphia Flyers assistant coach

REMARKABLE REARGUARDS

Tim Horton

Toronto, NY Rangers, Pittsburgh, Buffalo

An injury actually helped Tim Horton become one of the NHL's most remarkable rearguards. Horton was a promising player, but he made too many careless errors. Then, in March 1955, Horton suffered a broken leg and lost his spot in the lineup. He knew the only way to win it back was to improve his defensive play.

Since the leg injury decreased Horton's speed and mobility, he learned how to use his strength. He became expert at clearing opposing players away from the crease and stopping an offensive attack with a crunching bodycheck. These skills made Horton a remarkable rearguard.

A six-time All-Star and a two-time runner-up for the Norris Trophy, Horton received his greatest honor when he was inducted into the Hockey Hall of Fame in 1977.

"I think the strongest, toughest player in the NHL is Tim Horton. He's clean, but not mean."
PUNCH IMLACH, 1962
Toronto Maple Leafs general manager

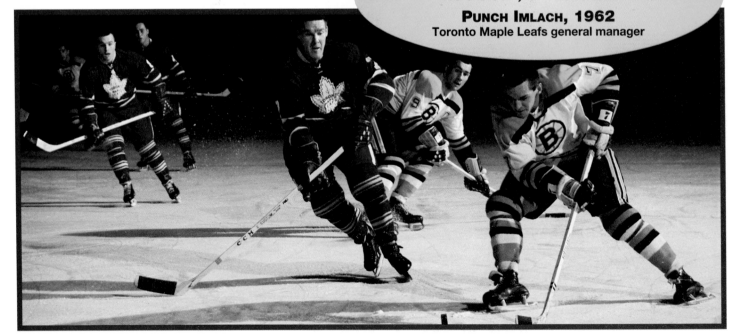

Guy Lapointe

Montreal, St. Louis, Boston

Guy Lapointe was a dependable defenseman who was effective on both sides of the blue line. He used his blistering shot from the point to become the only Montreal defenseman to score at least 20 goals in three straight seasons. In his own end, Lapointe was one of the best at blocking shots. He would wait until the shooter committed himself, then drop to the ice and block the shot with his shin pads.

Lapointe worked as hard in practice as he would in a game, and he expected the same dedication from his teammates. That devotion earned Lapointe five Stanley Cup rings and an honored place in the Hockey Hall of Fame.

"He has great mobility, a terrific shot, knows how to hit, and he's hungry to win."
AL MACNEIL, 1971
Montreal Canadiens coach

Lapointe's tough bodychecking made him a First Team All-Star in 1973.

THE ULTIMATE ALL-STAR

Ray Bourque

Boston

No defenseman in the history of the game of hockey has been as dominant as Boston's Ray Bourque. He has won the Norris Trophy for top defenseman five times and has scored at least 20 goals in a season nine times on his way to becoming the second highest-scoring defenseman ever in the NHL.

But there is much more to Bourque than statistics. He is one of the best at protecting his own zone, because he has so many weapons to get the job done. Bourque can win the battles in the corners with his strength. He's fast enough to skate the puck to safety, or he can find an opening through a jumble of skates and sticks to clear the puck.

One of the keys to Bourque's success is his approach to hockey. Even when things are going poorly on the ice, he tries to relax and enjoy the game. By not putting extra pressure on himself, Bourque can concentrate whenever he's on the ice. And that's important. Even at the age of 36, he still plays more minutes per game than anyone else on the team. The Boston Bruins' all-time leader in career assists, Bourque is the longest-serving captain currently playing in the NHL.

Although Bourque isn't big or fast, he's a top defenseman because he's one of the smartest players ever in the NHL.

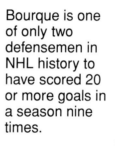

"When the other team has the puck in our end, he's the best defenseman who has ever played the game."
HARRY SINDEN, 1996
Boston Bruins general manager

Bourque is one of only two defensemen in NHL history to have scored 20 or more goals in a season nine times.

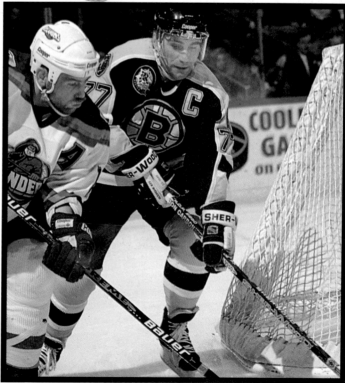

Rushing Russians

Viacheslav Fetisov

New Jersey, Detroit

The Russian hockey system has always depended on speed, skill, and surprise, and Viacheslav Fetisov excels at all of these. He uses his elegant skating to weave through the neutral zone and deliver a crisp pass to a teammate when the opposition least expects it. And when Fetisov can't find an open teammate, he has the speed to zoom to the net and create his own scoring opportunities.

Fetisov was already 31 when he joined the NHL's New Jersey Devils in 1989. Since then, he has used his knowledge and experience to improve his defensive zone coverage. Fetisov is an excellent shot-blocker and also has the offensive instincts of a forward.

> "Few defensemen see the entire ice as well as Fetisov. He makes great plays. He's unpredictable on offense and dependable on defense."
>
> **DAN BELISLE, 1995**
> **Detroit Red Wings scout**

Before he joined the NHL, Fetisov was selected to the Soviet National League All-Star Team nine times.

Sergei Zubov

NY Rangers, Pittsburgh, Dallas

Using his exceptional speed to burst through the opposing defense, Sergei Zubov loves to go end-to-end with the puck. He can accelerate in mid-stride, drop to a knee to intercept a pass, or break around a defender and still keep his balance. In 1993–94, Zubov led the Rangers in scoring and played a key role in the team's Stanley Cup victory.

Sergei Gonchar

Washington

Sergei Gonchar has learned to combine finesse with force. He has the speed to rush the puck and the skill to slip a pass through a clutter of skates. But Gonchar can also play a physical role behind the blue line. He has the size to force opposing forwards out of the zone, and the physical strength to win battles for rebounds and loose pucks.

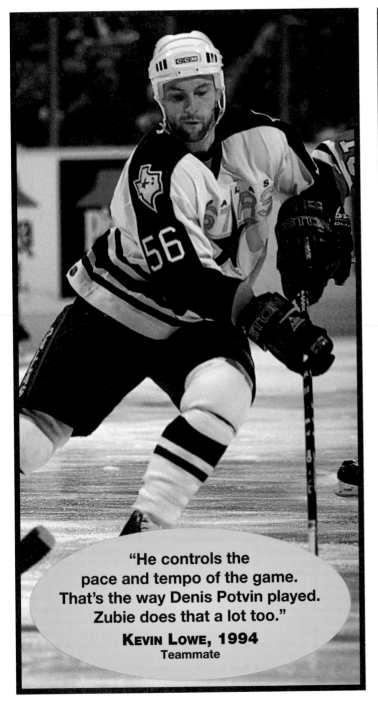

"He controls the pace and tempo of the game. That's the way Denis Potvin played. Zubie does that a lot too."

KEVIN LOWE, 1994
Teammate

"A solid positional player who's very effective with his fast and accurate passes. He handles himself well and is a leader on the ice."

NHL CENTRAL SCOUTING BUREAU, 1992

THE LEGENDS

Pierre Pilote

Chicago, Toronto

Pierre Pilote spent five years in the minors before making it to the NHL to stay. He used that time to gain confidence and to work on his stickhandling. When Pilote joined Chicago, he had the skill to lug the puck, defend his zone, and quarterback the power play. Pilote won the Norris Trophy in three straight years, from 1963 to 1965.

Leonard "Red" Kelly

Detroit, Toronto

Red Kelly played his position with the skill of a legend and the style of a gentleman. A masterful skater and stickhandler, Kelly was the backbone of the Detroit blue line for 13 seasons. He was the first defenseman in history to score at least 15 goals in seven straight seasons. Kelly won the Norris Trophy in 1954, the first time it was awarded.

"We couldn't honestly predict a future for him, because he was shy on size and skill. But he gritted his teeth and literally forced his way into the NHL."

TOMMY IVAN, 1961
Chicago Black Hawks
general manager

"Kelly attacks like a great forward and defends like an even greater defenseman. There's nobody like him for taking the pressure off his own team."

CARSON COOPER, 1953
NY Rangers scout

Eddie Shore

Boston, NY Americans

Known as the toughest defenseman ever, Eddie Shore was also one of the best. He had a legendary ability to play through pain and often played 60 minutes a night. Shore could also ignite the Bruins' offensive attack by carrying the puck end-to-end. Shore is the only defenseman to win the league MVP award four times, and was named to the NHL All-Star Team eight times.

Shore was one of the roughest players ever in the NHL. He was determined to win whenever he was on the ice.

"He would have been a star in any era. Eddie was a master at moving the puck. In the old days, defensemen usually hung back. Not Eddie."

LESTER PATRICK, 1948
Hall-of-Fame member

Francis "King" Clancy

Ottawa, Toronto

King Clancy was an expert at talking opponents into taking needless penalties or making mental mistakes. But he also had the skills to become one of the all-time great defensemen. Clancy could control the tempo of the game with his stickhandling and skating. A four-time All-Star, Clancy was inducted into the Hockey Hall of Fame in 1958.

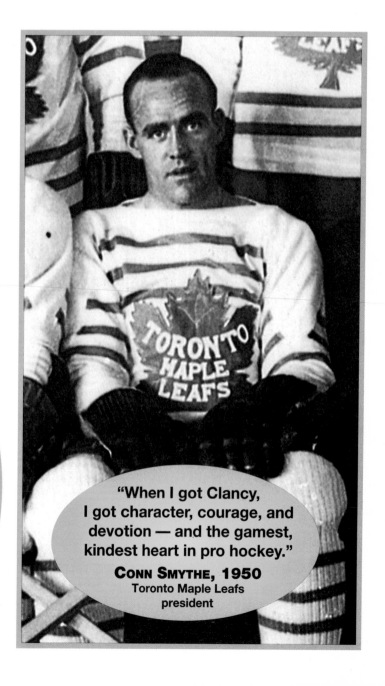

"When I got Clancy, I got character, courage, and devotion — and the gamest, kindest heart in pro hockey."

CONN SMYTHE, 1950
Toronto Maple Leafs president

DEDICATION AND DESIRE

Chris Chelios

Montreal, Chicago

One of hockey's most intense competitors, Chris Chelios is also one of the top blue-liners in the game. Few players can match his desire, dedication, and stamina. Chelios plays 35 to 40 minutes a game, delivering bone-crunching bodychecks while directing the Blackhawks attack.

Chelios is most effective at getting the puck out of his own zone. He can softly flip the puck off the glass or blast it around the boards. When those routes are covered, Chelios has the speed and skill to carry the puck on an end-to-end rush. One of only three defensemen to win the Norris Trophy with two different teams, Chelios was named to the World Cup of Hockey All-Star Team in the fall of 1996.

"When you watch Chris Chelios, you are watching the hardest-working individual in hockey, without exception."

MIKE KEENAN, 1996
St. Louis Blues general manager

Chelios is the first American-born defenseman to win the Norris Trophy three times.

Gary Suter

Calgary, Chicago

Extra effort and dedication have paid off for Gary Suter. Since he wasn't selected until the ninth round of the 1984 Entry Draft, Suter knew he needed to improve his strength and stamina. He worked so hard with the Flames in 1985–86 that he won the Calder Trophy as rookie of the year.

Suter is a strong skater and he keeps his shots from the point low and hard so his forwards can easily tip them. But more important is Suter's consistency on both sides of the blue line. He moves the puck with confidence, is one of the best at tying up opposing forwards in the crease, and is also one of the NHL's top playmakers.

"He's a very steady player who moves the puck well. He shoots the puck very well, and he's been a valuable addition to our team."

CLIFF FLETCHER, 1987
Calgary Flames
general manager

A member of the 1986 All-Rookie Team, Suter has recorded three 20-goal seasons in his NHL career.

THE MIRACLE WORKER

Bobby Orr

Boston, Chicago

When Harry Howell won the Norris Trophy in 1967, he said, "I'm glad I won it now, 'cause that young fellow in Boston will win it for the next ten years." That young fellow was Bobby Orr, and he changed the way defense is played.

Before Orr entered the league, a defenseman might skate the puck to the enemy blue line, but rarely would he join the attack inside the offensive end. However, Orr not only carried the puck into the attack zone, he stayed until he spotted an open teammate or found a clear path for a shot on net. Miraculously, Orr would be back in position to make a key defensive play — he always knew where to be on the ice. Those skills made Orr one of the greatest ever to play hockey.

When Orr joined the Boston Bruins in 1966, the team had missed the playoffs for seven straight seasons and had not won the Stanley Cup in 25 years. But with Orr directing the offense and leading the defense, the Bruins won two Stanley Cup titles. He was the first defenseman to collect 100 points in a season, and is still the only rearguard to win the Art Ross Trophy as the NHL's leading scorer. Orr also holds the record for most points scored by a defenseman in a single season.

Although Orr didn't win the Norris Trophy for ten straight years as Harry Howell predicted, he did win the award a record-setting eight consecutive times.

"Bobby Orr is one of a kind, a phenomenon. There has never been a hockey player like Bobby Orr and there never will be again."
HARRY SINDEN, 1971
Boston Bruins coach

Orr had outstanding speed and skated low to the ice, making it difficult for the opposition to knock him off his skates.

BLUE-LINE BLASTERS

Sandis Ozolinsh

San Jose, Colorado

Much of Sandis Ozolinsh's success in the NHL is due to his overpowering shot. Ozolinsh has developed a low, accurate slapshot that is easy for his teammates to deflect but difficult for opposing goalies to see through a crowd of sticks and skates.

Ozolinsh has great balance and can smoothly shift his weight from leg to leg as he shoots. By using a short backswing and snapping his wrists as he strikes the puck, Ozolinsh gets his shot away quickly. This combination of skills has made him a top blue-line blaster. While with San Jose, Ozolinsh set team records for most goals and points by a defenseman, and those records still stand.

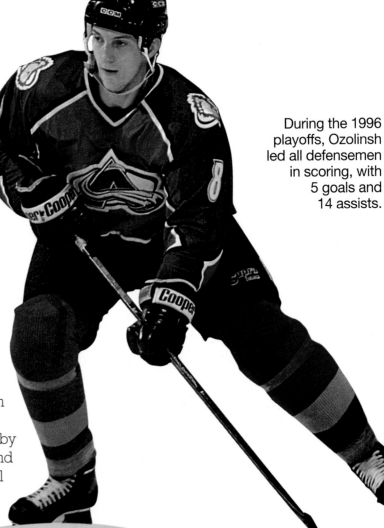

During the 1996 playoffs, Ozolinsh led all defensemen in scoring, with 5 goals and 14 assists.

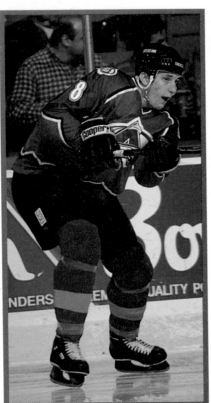

"He is genuinely trying to become a better defensive player, doing all the little things that help the team win."
KEVIN CONSTANTINE, 1995
San Jose Sharks coach

Doug Wilson

Chicago, San Jose

Early in his career, Doug Wilson had trouble getting his slapshot in the net. So he perfected the "snapshot," a wrist shot combined with a slapshot. By using a short backswing and quick follow-through, Wilson was able to improve his accuracy without losing speed. The snapshot also let him keep his head up so he could focus on where he wanted his shot to go. Wilson's shot was judged one of the best in the league at the time.

Wilson was also one of the NHL's best skaters. He could easily change speeds, move side-to-side, and skate backward. That combination of skating and shooting skills made Wilson one of the NHL's top defensemen during his 16-year career.

Wilson won the Norris Trophy in 1981–82 after scoring 39 goals, the fourth-highest single-season total by a defenseman in NHL history.

"If I had my choice on who could take a penalty shot, it would be Wilson. He has the most accurate wrist shot on the team."
ORVAL TESSIER, 1983
Chicago Black Hawks coach

DEPENDABLE DEFENDERS

Leo Boivin

Toronto, Boston, Detroit, Pittsburgh, Minnesota

One of the hardest-hitting rearguards of all time, Leo Boivin was nicknamed "Fireplug" because he was short but solid and muscular. A crafty hip-checker and a thundering bodychecker, Boivin was known as a "stay-at-home" defenseman. That meant he was at his best protecting his own zone and keeping opposing forwards away from his goaltender.

Sylvain Lefebvre

Montreal, Toronto, Quebec, Colorado

An expert at clearing the puck from his own zone, Sylvain Lefebvre is a tough checker and a confident stickhandler. Because he can remain cool in even the most pressure-packed situations and adapt to any defensive system, Lefebvre is rarely caught off guard. He's also one of the best in the league at forcing opposing forwards off the puck so his teammates can start an offensive attack.

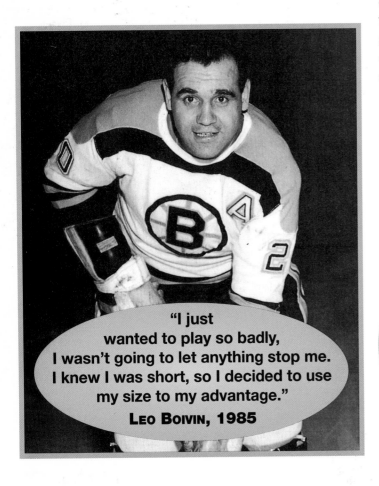

> "I just wanted to play so badly, I wasn't going to let anything stop me. I knew I was short, so I decided to use my size to my advantage."
> **LEO BOIVIN, 1985**

> "I take pride in what I do and how I play. It's encouraging that people see I make a contribution to the team even though I don't score a lot of goals or do fancy things."
> **SYLVAIN LEFEBVRE, 1994**

Adam Foote
Quebec, Colorado

Rod Langway
Montreal, Washington

Adam Foote is one of the "lunch-bucket" type of NHL defensemen — players who work hard every night and aren't often in the spotlight. The secrets to Foote's success are his footwork and skating speed. He can elude attackers, reach loose pucks, and clear the defensive zone. Foote's determined and physical style of play have made him one of the NHL's most dependable defenders.

One of the best American-trained rearguards to ever play hockey, Rod Langway concentrated on controlling the play behind the blue line. By using quick, sharp passes to clear the zone, Langway was able to keep the opposing forwards off guard. With his size and strength, he could also get very physical along the boards. Langway was named the NHL's top defenseman in 1983 and 1984.

"I'm more of a stay-at-home type because it takes a long time for a defenseman to develop in this league. I'm still learning. When I'm more comfortable, I'll start jumping into the play."
ADAM FOOTE, 1996

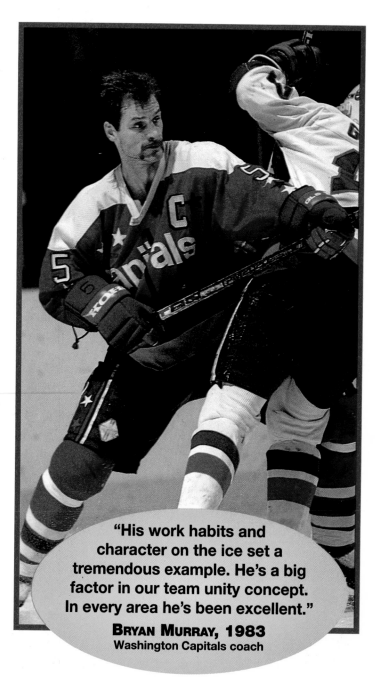

"His work habits and character on the ice set a tremendous example. He's a big factor in our team unity concept. In every area he's been excellent."
BRYAN MURRAY, 1983
Washington Capitals coach

STYLE AND SPEED

The third player selected in the 1991 Entry Draft, Niedermayer was a member of the 1993 NHL All-Rookie Team.

Scott Niedermayer

New Jersey

Scott Niedermayer's skating and puckhandling have made him one of the NHL's elite young players. In his third full NHL season, Niedermayer played a key role in New Jersey's first Stanley Cup title, and in 1996 he played for Team Canada in the World Cup of Hockey.

Niedermayer's effortless skating allows him to play a mature, confident game. He can speed up quickly or turn sharply without losing his balance. Unlike many young defensemen, Niedermayer can also stickhandle well in traffic. He has the confidence to hang on to the puck while killing penalties or setting up the power play. This allows his teammates to get into position to accept a pass or create a scoring opportunity.

"When he went back to the basics — making the plays without trying to rush the puck all night — he became a better player."

NICK POLANO, 1995
Calgary Flames
pro scout

Scott Stevens

Washington, St. Louis, New Jersey

The key to Scott Stevens's style is his physical presence. He has the size to overpower players in the slot and deliver solid bodychecks along the boards. And Stevens has the strength and stamina to play 30 to 35 minutes a game without losing his effectiveness. Stevens is also an agile skater. He has excellent acceleration forward, backward, and sideways.

On offense, Stevens creates scoring opportunities with his patience. He will hold on to the puck until his forwards can break free of their checkers. And while his shot from the point is not overpowering, he keeps it low so it can easily be tipped in by his teammates. Stevens scored a career-high 21 goals in 1984–85.

A three-time NHL All-Star, Stevens finished as runner-up for the Norris Trophy in 1987–88 and 1993–94.

"The first thing that stood out about Scott was his strong physical play. He wasn't afraid to hit people."
DAVID POILE, 1994
Washington Capitals general manager

THE NATURAL

Paul Coffey

**Edmonton, Pittsburgh, Los Angeles,
Detroit, Hartford, Philadelphia**

Three things set Paul Coffey apart from other defensemen: skating, stickhandling, and shooting. Since he joined the NHL in 1980, Coffey has been one of the league's fastest skaters. Most of his speed comes naturally, but Coffey has some secrets to give him a better feel for the ice. Early in his career, Coffey wore skates that were too small. The tight fit let him push off with extra power. Also, Coffey has his skate blades specially sharpened to give him better balance and help him glide faster and farther.

Another advantage Coffey has is his ability to stickhandle through a crowd of players. His excellent puck control makes it seem as if he has the puck on a string. If you watch Coffey as he bursts up the ice with the puck, you'll notice he never has to look down. A lightweight stick helps give him a special feel for the puck.

Coffey has a wide variety of shots, and he's one of the best at shooting while in full flight. He's also an expert at feathering a pass through a maze of players or slamming a set-up to the lip of the goal crease. Coffey's ability to anticipate the play and his speed have earned him nine selections to the NHL All-Star Team. He's the NHL's all-time leader in goals, assists, and points by a defenseman. In December 1996 Coffey was traded to Philadelphia.

Coffey is the only defenseman to score 40 goals in a season twice and the first to record 1000 assists. He has won the Norris Trophy three times — in 1985, 1986, and 1995.

"Paul's the best passing defenseman in the game. He reads the play well and he has great mobility. He glides faster than most players skate."

JOHN MUCKLER, 1991
Edmonton Oilers coach

THE PLAYMAKERS

"He picks his spots and openings perfectly. Too many defensemen take blind shots. Not Brad. His shots are never blocked and never miss the net."

LARRY POPEIN, 1972
Teammate

Brad Park

NY Rangers, Boston, Detroit

Brad Park was one of the most gifted defensemen ever to play the game. Although he was solid defensively, Park was best known for his offensive instincts and his ability to set up scoring chances. Unlike many of the blue-liners in his era who fed their teammates long passes to set up scoring chances, Park carried the puck from end to end.

Park would speed into the attacking zone, controlling the puck until he spotted an opportunity. Then he would slip a feed to a charging forward or drill a low shot toward a teammate stationed near the edge of the crease for an easy tip-in. Those talents enabled Park to record 683 career assists, the sixth-highest total in NHL history among defensemen.

A nine-time NHL All-Star, Park won the Masterton Trophy in 1984 for perseverance, sportsmanship, and dedication to hockey.

Phil Housley

Buffalo, Winnipeg, St. Louis, Calgary,
New Jersey, Washington

Only four players in hockey history have gone directly from high school to the NHL, and Phil Housley is the only defenseman to make that jump. By the age of 18, he had already developed exceptional stickhandling and passing skills. Most important, Housley was a poised and confident player, and he adapted quickly to NHL play.

Housley has an incredible ability to spot openings on the ice — an open passing lane, for instance, or a player who's free to receive a pass. And once he's spotted an opening, he has the talent to do something about it. This playmaker can put a long pass right onto the blade of a forward's stick or flip a delicate pass past an opponent.

> "He's got all the instincts. He knows when to jump into the play and when to stay back. You can't teach that. That's a gift."
>
> **CRAIG JANNEY, 1993**
> Teammate

Housley is the fifth-highest-scoring defenseman in NHL history.

STANLEY CUP SUPERSTARS

Larry Robinson

Montreal, Los Angeles

Larry Robinson appeared in more Stanley Cup playoff games than any defenseman in NHL history. "The Big Bird" made 20 consecutive trips to the playoffs, and came away with a Stanley Cup title six times. With his long reach, Robinson could intercept passes and break up scoring chances. He also excelled at setting up scoring chances for his own team.

In the 1978 playoffs, Robinson led all playoff performers with 17 assists, and tied for the postseason scoring lead with 21 points. That earned him the Conn Smythe Trophy as the playoffs' most valuable player.

A six-time All-Star, Robinson won the Norris Trophy as the NHL's top rearguard twice, in 1977 and 1980.

"He was the rare player whose effect on the game was far greater than any statistical contribution he might make."
KEN DRYDEN, 1980
Teammate

Serge Savard

Montreal, Winnipeg

Serge Savard is best remembered for inventing the "Savardian spinnerama." He would wait inside the attacking zone for an opposing player to reach him. Then Savard would spin away from the defender and drive to the net. He also used his spinnerama to elude forecheckers. Savard's unique style earned him a place in the Hockey Hall of Fame.

> "I've never seen a man of his size stop and turn so quickly. Right now, he's the Canadiens' best defenseman."
> **DAVE KEON, 1970**
> Toronto Maple Leafs center

Savard won the Stanley Cup seven times as a player and twice as a general manager. He also won the Conn Smythe Trophy as the most valuable player in the 1969 playoffs.

Al MacInnis

Calgary, St. Louis

No player today can shoot the puck like big Al MacInnis. With his strong wrists, he can fire the puck at speeds well over 100 miles per hour! That shot helped MacInnis make Stanley Cup history in 1989. He became the first defenseman to lead the postseason scoring race, and won the Conn Smythe Trophy as playoff MVP.

> "With MacInnis, everybody talks heart and soul. He's been on a Stanley Cup winner and knows what it takes to get to the finals."
> **JACK QUINN, 1995**
> St. Louis Blues president and CEO

MacInnis was the runner-up to Ray Bourque in the Norris Trophy race in 1990 and 1991.

THE PIONEERS

Reed Larson

Detroit, Boston, Edmonton, NY Islanders, Minnesota, Buffalo

Reed Larson was the first American-born defenseman to come out of the U.S. college system and become an offensive star in the NHL. He could play any position, and was often used as a forward on the power play. Unlike some rearguards, Larson had the strength to dig the puck out of the corners and the toughness to position himself in the slot for a scoring opportunity.

Thanks to a slapshot that was timed at 110 miles per hour, Larson became the highest-scoring defenseman in Red Wings history. He is still the only American-born defenseman to score at least 20 goals in five straight seasons.

> "I can play him on the wing and still have him back on defense in crucial situations."
>
> **BOBBY KROMM, 1980**
> **Detroit Red Wings coach**

While studying at the University of Minnesota, Larson was drafted by Detroit. He turned pro with the Red Wings in 1976.

Borje Salming
Toronto, Detroit

Many experts thought that Borje Salming would never make it in the NHL. In his first few years in the league, everyone challenged him to prove he could handle the NHL's rugged style. So Salming responded by never backing down on the ice.

Salming also paid special attention to physical conditioning and perfected his stickhandling skills. That allowed this Swedish star to play both the gritty checking game and the freewheeling offensive style that best suited his talent. In 1996 this pioneer became the first European-trained defenseman to be inducted into the Hockey Hall of Fame.

"You knew when you played Toronto that Borje would be in your face. He was the defenseman we all worried about."
MIKE BOSSY, 1996
Hall-of-Fame forward

Salming earned six consecutive All-Star berths and is the all-time leading scorer among rearguards in Toronto Maple Leaf history.

THE ALL-AMERICAN

Brian Leetch

NY Rangers

Brian Leetch has been an All-American ever since he started playing hockey. The top defenseman with Boston College in 1986–87, Leetch went on to play for the U.S. Olympic team at the 1988 Winter Games. Then he joined the Rangers and has been one of the NHL's best defensemen ever since.

Speed and good reflexes are the keys to Leetch's success. Everything starts with his ability to quickly read any on-ice situation and react to it by making fast, accurate decisions under pressure. Leetch is able to make them work because his quick feet and hands allow him to get the jump on an opponent to clear the zone or spot a scoring opportunity.

Leetch has the ability to control the game every time he is on the ice. He can deliberately slow the pace by ragging the puck to give his team time to regroup. Or he can speed up the game by suddenly bursting out of his own zone to lead a four-man rush up the ice. Another remarkable quality of Leetch's play is his ability to anticipate. He is able to determine where the puck is going to be before it gets there. That's one of the big reasons Leetch has consistently been an All-American.

"Leetch is so great offensively. When he comes over the blue line, you can be sure something is going to happen. He's just a tremendous talent."

KEVIN PRENDERGAST, 1992
Edmonton Oilers director of hockey operations

One of the highlights of Leetch's career came in 1996 when he was named captain of Team USA at the World Cup of Hockey.

The 1992 Norris Trophy winner, Leetch was selected as the playoff MVP in 1994.

THE RECORD BREAKERS

Larry Murphy

Los Angeles, Washington, Minnesota, Pittsburgh, Toronto

Larry Murphy became a record breaker in his very first NHL season. In 1980–81, he recorded 60 assists and 76 points for the Los Angeles Kings. No rookie defenseman has yet been able to surpass Murphy's incredible marks.

Although he isn't a graceful skater and does not have an overpowering shot, Murphy has lasted 18 seasons in the NHL. His endurance is due to his durability and his attention to detail. Murphy studies every aspect of the game, and that preparation helps him anticipate plays and take advantage of his opponents' weaknesses. Thanks to a rigorous fitness program, Murphy has never missed more than five games in a season.

"What you see with Larry Murphy is what you get. He controls the power play, he's a stable defenseman, he's exactly what we knew he would be."
PAT BURNS, 1996
Toronto Maple Leafs coach

A three-time NHL Second Team All-Star, Murphy is the fourth NHL defenseman to record 1000 career points.

Denis Potvin

NY Islanders

Before he even made it to the NHL, Denis Potvin was already a record breaker. In junior hockey, Potvin collected 123 points in a single season to set a new mark for points by a defenseman.

Few defensemen had as many offensive weapons as Potvin. He could speed around a checker, muscle a defender off the puck, or drive a slapshot home for a goal. But even more important, Potvin kept himself healthy and in shape, and had the ability to play with pain. That enabled him to score at least 15 goals in 12 of his 15 years in the league. A three-time winner of the Norris Trophy, Potvin broke all of Bobby Orr's career scoring records and became the first defenseman to record 1000 points.

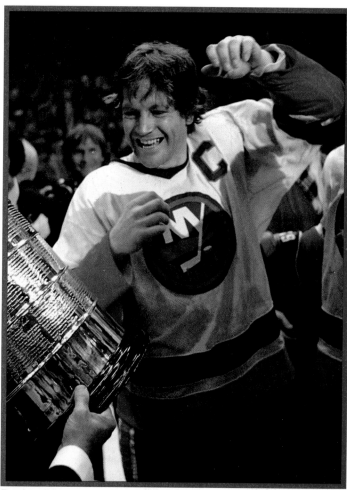

During his career, Potvin scored two overtime goals that won important games, including the first match-up of the 1980 finals against Philadelphia.

"I was able to break Bobby Orr's records because of good luck, good health, and longevity."
DENIS POTVIN, 1986

Potvin set and broke records throughout his career and was an All-Star seven times.

ON THE RISE

Bryan Berard

NY Islanders

Bryan Berard has all the tools to become a dominant defenseman in the NHL. Creative on offense and tough on defense, he can lay on the muscle to move forwards out of the slot and away from the crease. Berard was chosen first overall in the 1995 Entry Draft.

Wade Redden

Ottawa

One of the NHL's top new talents, Wade Redden is a natural on-ice leader who plays clean but tough. In his rookie season, Redden proved he had the confidence and skill to take chances on offense, plus the speed and maturity to improve his skills on defense.

Oleg Tverdovsky

Anaheim, Winnipeg, Phoenix

Now in his fourth NHL season, Oleg Tverdovsky emerged as one of the NHL's top young defensemen in 1996-97. With his outstanding skating and passing skills, he has become the offensive anchor of the Phoenix Coyotes blue-line crew.